Hot & Spicy Cookbook

40 Hot and Spicy Recipes That Will Light Up Your Tastebuds

BY: Nancy Silverman

COPYRIGHT NOTICES

© 2019 Nancy Silverman All Rights Reserved

Subject to the agreement and permission of the author, this Book, in part or in whole, may not be reproduced in any format. This includes but is not limited to electronically, in print, scanning or photocopying.

The opinions, guidelines and suggestions written here are solely those of the Author and are for information purposes only. Every possible measure has been taken by the Author to ensure accuracy but let the Reader be advised that they assume all risk when following information. The Author does not assume any risk in the case of damages, personally or commercially, in the case of misinterpretation or misunderstanding while following any part of the Book.

My Heartfelt Thanks and A Special Reward for Your Purchase!

https://nancy.gr8.com

My heartfelt thanks at purchasing my book and I hope you enjoy it! As a special bonus, you will now be eligible to receive books absolutely free on a weekly basis! Get started by entering your email address in the box above to subscribe. A notification will be emailed to you of my free promotions, no purchase necessary! With little effort, you will be eligible for free and discounted books daily. In addition to this amazing gift, a reminder will be sent 1-2 days before the offer expires to remind you not to miss out. Enter now to start enjoying this special offer!

Table of Contents

Chapter I – Entrees 8

(1) Sticky Pineapple Chicken Stir Fry.................................. 9

(2) Sticky Orange Ginger Chicken 12

(3) Ultimate Chicken Soup 15

(4) Chipotle-Spiked Mustard Salmon 18

(5) Spicy Stuffed Whiskey Turkey Burgers........................ 20

(6) Chocolate Chili.. 23

(7) Spicy Lime Chicken.. 26

(8) Eggs in Minted Tomato Sauce 29

(9) Roasted Vegetable Pizza with Ghost Pepper Sauce 32

(10) Horseradish and Wasabi Firecracker Snapper 36

(11) Lamb Vindaloo... 38

(12) Hot Pepper Sloppy Joes... 41

Chapter II - Appetizers, Dips and Sides........................... 44

(13) Wasabi Crab Patties 45

(14) Cajun Wings 48

(15) Hot 'n Spicy Crab Dip 51

(16) Spicy Welsh Rarebit 53

(17) Curried Coconut Egg Drop Soup 56

(18) Spicy Bacon-Wrapped Shrimp 58

(19) Firecracker Chicken Meatballs 61

(20) Spiced Spinach and Onion Pakoras 64

(21) Honey Ginger Shrimp 67

(22) Prawn Puri 69

(23) Horseradish Cream Cheese with Fruit Dip 72

(24) Mexican Chili Grilled Corn 74

(25) Horseradish Deviled Eggs 77

(26) Jalapeño Poppers 79

(27) Hot Artichoke and Spinach Dip 82

Chapter III – Dessert 85

(28) Cranberry-Jalapeño Granita 86

(29) Wasabi Pea Chocolate Bark 88

(30) Apple Dutch Baby with Green Chilis 90

(31) Tequila Grilled Watermelon 93

(32) Black Pepper Ice-Cream 95

(33) Strawberry and Jalapeño Gin Popsicles 98

(34) Cardamom and Vanilla Ice Cream 100

(35) Spicy Peanut Popcorn 104

(36) Chocolate Chili Pots 108

(37) Fire Roasted Pears 111

(38) Chocolate Dipped Coconut Curry Macaroons 114

(39) Dark Chocolate Jalapeño Bread Pudding 118

(40) Chocolate Dipped Strawberries 121

About the Author 124

Author's Afterthoughts 126

Chapter I – Entrees

(1) Sticky Pineapple Chicken Stir Fry

This sweet, spicy, fruity chicken is a guaranteed crowd pleaser. Serve with rice for a delicious and quick dinner.

Serving Size: 4

Preparation Time: 10 minutes

Total Cooking Time: 8 hours 30 minutes

Ingredient List:

- 8 ounces canned pineapple
- ⅓ cup soy sauce
- ⅓ cup molasses
- 3 tablespoons malt vinegar
- 1 tablespoon tomato ketchup
- 2 tablespoons chili sauce
- 2 garlic cloves (crushed)
- ½ teaspoon fresh ginger (grated)
- 2 pounds chicken breast (cubed)
- 3 tablespoons canola oil
- Red pepper flakes (for garnish)

Instructions:

1. In a blender, mix the pineapple, soy sauce, molasses, malt vinegar, tomato ketchup, chili sauce, crushed garlic, and grated ginger. Blitz until totally combined.
2. Add the chicken to a large bowl and cover with the marinade. Toss well to coat completely. Cover and refrigerate for 6 hours.
3. Heat the oil in a pan until 'popping'. Add the chicken and marinade to the pan and sauté until the chicken is cooked through and the marinade has reduced to a very sticky glaze. Serve immediately with rice and a sprinkling of red pepper flakes.

(2) Sticky Orange Ginger Chicken

Now you can enjoy one of your favorite Asian takeout dishes without any nasty ingredients, all in the comfort of your own home.

Serving Size: 4

Preparation Time: 10 minutes

Total Cooking Time: 1hour 25 minutes

Ingredient List:

- 1¼ cups fresh squeezed orange juice
- ¼ cup soy sauce (low sodium)
- 3 tablespoons fresh ginger (grated)
- 2 tablespoons fresh garlic (minced)
- 2 tablespoons olive oil
- 2 tablespoons chili sauce
- 1½ tablespoon rice vinegar
- 2 teaspoons brown sugar
- 2 teaspoons orange zest
- ½ teaspoon white pepper
- 1½ pounds chicken breast (cut into strips)
- 1 tablespoon cornstarch
- 1 tablespoon water
- ¼ cup green onions (sliced)
- Rice (for serving)

Instructions:

1. Combine the juice, soy sauce, grated ginger, minced garlic, olive oil (one tablespoon), chili sauce, rice vinegar, brown sugar, and orange zest in a bowl. Stir until well combined.
2. Add the chicken strips into a resealable zipper bag and pour a third of a cup of the marinade over it. Use your hands to gently massage the bag, ensuring that the chicken is well coated. Refrigerate for an hour.
3. Heat the remaining olive oil in a skillet over high heat. Add the chicken (discarding the marinade) and sauté for just over 5 minutes, until browned and just cooked. Take out chicken and set aside.
4. Turn the heat down and pour the reserved marinade into the skillet. Bring to a boil.
5. In a small bowl combine the cornstarch and water and stir well. Add the mixture to the skillet.
6. Use a whisk to stir the sauce, ensuring the cornstarch is totally incorporated. Boil for another minute before returning the chicken to the skillet. Cook for a final 2-3 minutes until the chicken is completely cooked through and hot.
7. Serve immediately with rice and a sprinkling of green onions.

(3) Ultimate Chicken Soup

Feeling a little under the weather? Then this fresh and healthy soup, packed with vitamins and minerals, is just what you need.

Serving Size: 4

Preparation Time: 5 minutes

Total Cooking Time: 20 minutes

Ingredient List:

- 4 cups spicy chicken broth
- 2 pounds squash (cut into small chunks)
- 2 cups savoy cabbage (chopped into wedges)
- 2 cups bok choy (chopped into wedges)
- 4 cups cooked chicken (shredded)
- Sea salt and black pepper (to taste)
- 1 fresh jalapeño (sliced)
- Fresh cilantro, basil (torn for garnish)
- Chili oil (for serving)
- 1 piece ginger (2 inches, grated)
- 3 fresh limes (sliced into wedges)

Instructions:

1. Pour the broth into a large pot and place over medium heat. Throw in the squash and bring to a simmer for 9-10 minutes.
2. Add the wedges of savoy cabbage, bok choy, and chicken; allow to simmer for another 4-5 minutes until heated through. Season to taste with sea salt and black pepper.
3. Ladle the soup evenly into warmed bowls.
4. Top each equally with slices of jalapeño and sprinkle over the fresh cilantro and basil. Finish with a drizzle of chili oil and a pinch of grated ginger.
5. Serve immediately with the lime wedges.

(4) Chipotle-Spiked Mustard Salmon

Horseradish, mustard, and chipotle pepper work together to give these salmon fillets a sensational, spicy flavor.

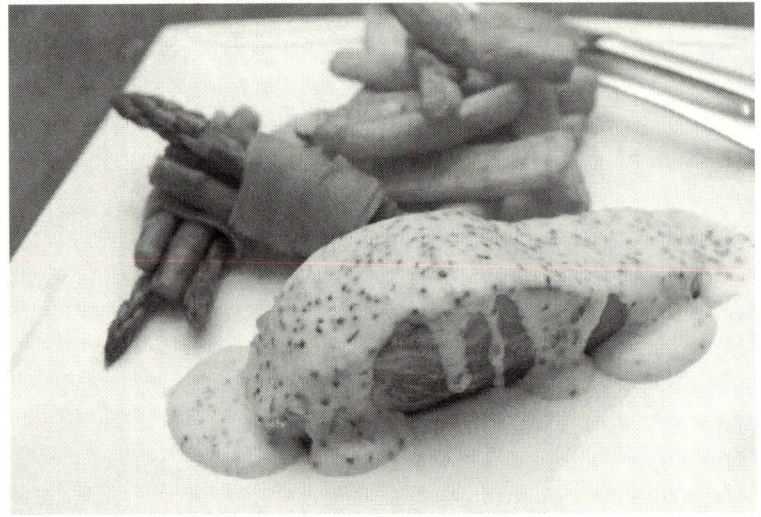

Serving Size: 6

Preparation Time: 5 minutes

Total Cooking Time: 25 minutes

Ingredient List:

- ¼ cup reduced fat mayonnaise
- ¼ cup prepared horseradish
- ¼ cup mustard
- ¼ teaspoon lemon-pepper seasoning
- 1 teaspoon minced chipotle pepper in adobo sauce
- 6 (4 ounce) salmon fillets
- 1 teaspoon fresh dill

Instructions:

1. Preheat the main oven to 350 degrees F. Line a large baking tin with aluminum foil and place the fillets on it.
2. In a medium mixing bowl, mix the mayonnaise, horseradish, mustard, lemon seasoning, and chipotle pepper and evenly spread on each of the salmon fillets.
3. Transfer the baking tin to the preheated oven for 15-20 minutes or until the salmon flakes easily when tested with a fork.
4. Serve sprinkled with dill.

(5) Spicy Stuffed Whiskey Turkey Burgers

Always wear gloves when handling hot peppers. Avoid contact with eyes and don't be tempted to pop a whole one in your mouth—enjoy these hot and spicy burgers responsibly!

Serving Size: 2

Preparation Time: 10 minutes

Total Cooking Time: 40 minutes

Ingredient List:

- 14 ounces ground turkey
- 2 tablespoons breadcrumbs
- ¼ cup whiskey (top shelf)
- 2 tablespoons Worcestershire
- 2 tablespoons roasted garlic
- For the stuffing
- 1 yellow Ghost pepper (deseeded, chopped)
- 1 teaspoon good quality whiskey (top shelf)
- 2 tablespoons goat cheese
- 1 tablespoon hot chili powder
- 2 burger buns (sliced open)

Instructions:

1. In a large mixing bowl, combine the ground turkey, breadcrumbs, ¼ cup of good quality whiskey, Worcestershire sauce, and roasted garlic. Carefully mix by hand.

2. Wearing disposable gloves, mold the turkey mixture into 4 patties of equal size, and flatten to make a burger shape using the palm of your hand.
3. In a second bowl, add the chopped ghost pepper to the single teaspoon of good quality whiskey, hot chili powder and goat cheese. Stir well to ensure all the ingredients are combined.
4. Place half of the goat cheese mixture (1 tablespoon) onto one of the individual burgers. Place another burger over the mixture and then pinch the edges all the way around to seal the goat cheese inside, making a turkey-goat cheese patty. Repeat the process with the remaining patties.
5. Lightly oil your grill and bring to medium-high heat. Sear each stuffed burger for approximately 1-2 minutes on each side. Reduce the heat to medium. Allow the burgers to grill for 10-15 minutes, or until they are thoroughly cooked.
6. Serve in burger buns. Beware they will be hot and spicy!

(6) Chocolate Chili

Surprisingly, chocolate adds depth of flavor and a little sweetness to spicy chili dishes.

Serving Size: 8-10

Preparation Time: 10 minutes

Total Cooking Time: 1 hour 20 minutes

Ingredient List:

- 2 pounds ground beef
- 2 onions (chopped)
- 1 tablespoon ground cumin
- 2 tablespoons unsweetened cocoa powder
- 1½ tablespoon chili powder
- 3 cloves garlic (minced)
- 2 jalapeños (seeded, minced)
- 30 ounces ranch style beans (any brand)
- 1 teaspoon cayenne pepper
- 1 teaspoon dried oregano
- 30 ounces black beans (rinsed, drained)
- 15 ounces diced tomatoes
- 2 cups beef broth
- 4 cups tomato sauce
- Cheddar cheese (grated)

Instructions:

1. In a large pot over medium heat, cook the beef for 2-3 minutes. Then, stir in the chopped onions, ground cumin, cocoa powder, and chili powder, and cook for 2 minutes. Continue to stir while adding the minced garlic and jalapeño peppers. Stir for 1 minute to combine all of these ingredients.
2. Next, add the ranch style beans, cayenne pepper, and oregano. Continue to cook for 2 minutes.
3. Finally add the black beans, diced tomatoes, beef broth, and tomato sauce. Stir well.
4. Cover the dish and simmer for 50-60 minutes.
5. Sprinkle with grated Cheddar cheese prior to serving.

(7) Spicy Lime Chicken

Relatively quick to make. A lot of herbs and spices give this chicken dish its zesty taste. Ideal served with rice or a dinner salad.

Serving Size: 4

Preparation Time: 5 minutes

Total Cooking Time: 25 minutes

Ingredient List:

- ¾ teaspoon sea salt
- ¼ teaspoon fresh black pepper
- ⅛ teaspoon paprika
- ¼ teaspoon cayenne pepper
- ¼ teaspoon onion powder
- ¼ teaspoon garlic powder
- ¼ teaspoon dried thyme
- ¼ teaspoon dried parsley
- 4 boneless, chicken breast halves (skinned)
- 1 tablespoon virgin oil
- 2 tablespoons butter
- 2 teaspoons garlic powder
- 3 tablespoons fresh lime juice

Instructions:

1. In a small mixing bowl, combine the first 8 ingredients. Coat the chicken breast halves on both sides with the herb mixture.
2. In a skillet, heat the oil and butter over medium heat. Sauté the breasts until golden—this should take 5-6 minute on each side. Sprinkle each breast with 2 teaspoonss of garlic powder and fresh lime juice. Cook for a further 4-5 minutes, stirring continuously to ensure that the chicken is evenly coated with sauce.
3. The chicken is cooked when its juices run clear. Serve and enjoy!

(8) Eggs in Minted Tomato Sauce

A great dish packed with flavor. Place in the center of the table with some crusty bread and let everyone dig in.

Serving Size: 3-4

Preparation Time: 5 minutes

Total Cooking Time: 45 minutes

Ingredient List:

- 1 teaspoon butter
- 1 teaspoon olive oil
- 1 yellow onion (finely chopped)
- 1 jalapeño (deseeded and chopped)
- 4 garlic cloves (finely chopped)
- 1 (14 ounce) can chopped tomatoes
- ½ teaspoon hot sauce
- 1 bay leaf
- 1 tablespoon fresh mint (roughly chopped)
- 4 medium eggs
- Salt and black pepper (to taste)
- Crusty bread (for serving)

Instructions:

1. In a skillet, heat the butter and olive oil until butter has melted. Add the onion and sauté for 5 minutes, until softened.
2. Toss in the jalapeño and garlic and cook for another minute. Add the canned tomatoes along with a dash of hot sauce and the bay leaf. Allow to simmer for approximately 25-30 minutes, until thickened.
3. Sprinkle with the mint and then make 4 small wells with a spoon. Crack an egg into each of the 4 wells. Season to taste with salt and pepper and cook until the eggs are prepared to your liking.
4. Serve in the skillet with chunks of fresh crusty bread!

(9) Roasted Vegetable Pizza with Ghost Pepper Sauce

Ghost peppers are ranked as one of the hottest peppers on the Scoville scale—the way peppers are measured for spicy heat. You have been warned!

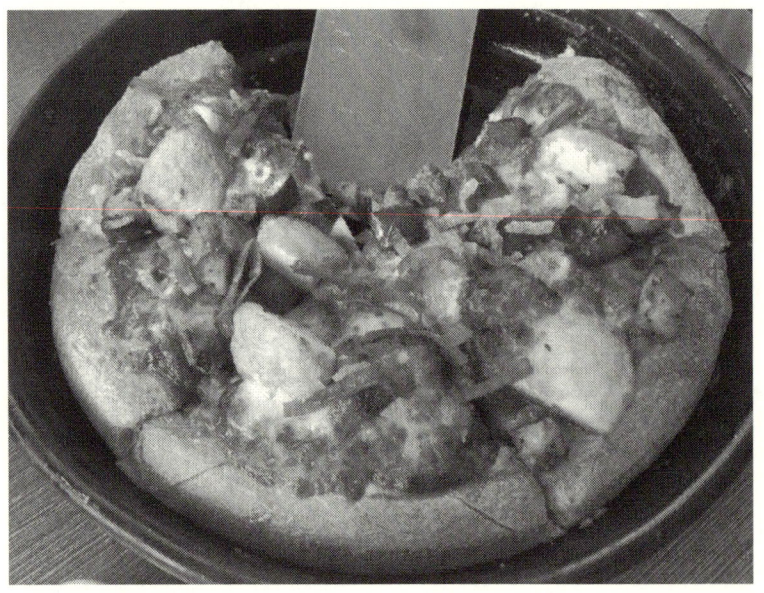

Serving Size: 1

Preparation Time: 30 minutes

Total Cooking Time: 1 hour 30 minutes

Ingredient List:

Roasted vegetables

- 1 large zucchini (halved, sliced)
- 1 large red onion (chopped)
- 8 ounces mushrooms (sliced)
- 1 pint cherry tomatoes
- 1 green pepper (chopped)
- 1 large carrot
- Handful of fresh green beans (trimmed)
- Salt and pepper
- ½ tsp garlic powder
- Olive oil

Ghost pepper sauce

- 1 ghost pepper (halved, seeded, minced)
- 1 can of diced tomatoes
- 2 tablespoons olive oil
- ½ tsp dried oregano
- ½ cup fresh basil (chopped)
- ¼ tsp black pepper
- 3 garlic cloves (minced)
- 1 tsp sugar

Pizza

- 1 readymade (12 inch) pizza dough
- 1 cup Cheddar cheese (shredded)
- Fresh Parmesan cheese (grated)
- ¼ cup jarred hot pepper rings (chopped)

Instructions:

1. Preheat the main oven to 425 degrees F. Line two rimless baking trays or sheets with greaseproof paper.
2. In a bowl, combine all of the vegetables. Sprinkle with salt, pepper and garlic powder and toss. Spread them out in a single layer on the baking trays and drizzle with olive oil.
3. Roast the vegetables in the preheated oven for 20 minutes. Remove from oven and toss to ensure that the oil coats all of the vegetables. Put back in the oven and cook for a further 8-10 minutes. Set aside.

4. To make the sauce: In a frying pan or skillet, combine all 8 sauce ingredients. Using medium heat, Bring the sauce to a boil before reducing to a simmer. Allow to simmer for 25-30 minutes, until the liquid begins to reduce. Remove the sauce from the heat and blitz in a food processor until silky.
5. Increase the heat of the oven to 475 degrees F and wait for it to be fully heated.
6. Spoon the sauce onto the prepared pizza crust. Next, layer the vegetables. Scatter with grated Cheddar cheese and Parmesan.
7. Place in the oven and cook for 12-15 minutes. The crust should be golden brown, the base crispy and the cheeses bubbling. Garnish with pepper rings prior to serving.

(10) Horseradish and Wasabi Firecracker Snapper

Did you know that horseradish is a member of the mustard family? Coupled with wasabi, this dish is sensationally spicy. Not for the faint of heart!

Serving Size: 4

Preparation Time: 10 minutes

Total Cooking Time: 50 minutes

Ingredient List:

- Juice of 1 fresh lime
- Zest of 1 fresh lime
- ¼ cup horseradish sauce
- 1 tablespoon wasabi powder
- 4 (8 ounce) red snapper fillets
- Flour
- Salt and black pepper

Instructions:

1. In a large baking or shallow casserole dish, combine the lime juice, zest, horseradish, and wasabi. Add the red snapper and allow to marinade for 30 minutes.
2. Remove the fish from the dish and drain off any excess marinade into a bowl. Set the marinade aside for later. Sprinkle the fish with salt and black pepper. Dust each side of the snapper with flour.
3. Using a large skillet, sauté the fish for 3-4 minutes on each side. Deglaze the skillet with the marinade and pour over the cooked fish. Enjoy!

(11) Lamb Vindaloo

Red hot chili pepper, Scotch bonnet, and Madras curry powder; if this recipe doesn't make your eyes water, nothing will.

Serving Size: 6-8

Preparation Time: 10 minutes

Total Cooking Time: 25 minutes

Ingredient List:

- 2 tablespoons ghee
- 1 teaspoon turmeric
- 2 scotch bonnet chillies (finely chopped)
- 1 tablespoon cumin powder
- 1 tablespoon coriander powder
- 1 tablespoon Madras curry powder
- 3 tablespoons red hot chili powder
- 1 bay leaf
- 6 green cardamom pods (smashed)
- 2 tablespoons garlic and ginger paste
- 4 cloves of garlic (chopped)
- 3 fresh green chilies (finely chopped)
- 2 potatoes (pre-boiled, roughly chopped)
- 2 cups heated curry sauce
- 2 pounds pre-cooked lamb meat
- 2 tablespoons plain yogurt
- 2 tablespoons vinegar
- 1 tablespoon tomato paste
- 3 tablespoons cilantro (chopped)
- Salt and black pepper

Instructions:

1. In a large, heavy frying pan, heat the ghee over a medium to high heat. Allow the ghee to sizzle for 1-2 minutes, then add all of the other spices. Next, add the garlic and ginger paste along with the 4 cloves of garlic. Stir well, and add the chopped chillies.
2. Add the potatoes and the curry sauce (previously heated). Stir well and ensure that the curry mixture is well combined. Add the precooked lamb pieces to the pan.
3. Gradually add yogurt to the mixture, continuously stirring to combine. Then, add the vinegar and tomato paste.
4. When you are satisfied with the seasonings, scatter with chopped cilantro and sprinkle with salt and black pepper.
5. Enjoy with rice.

(12) Hot Pepper Sloppy Joes

Sloppy Joes were created around 1940, but it's doubtful that the original recipe included hot peppers!

Serving Size: 4-6

Preparation Time: 10 minutes

Total Cooking Time: 50 minutes

Ingredient List:

- 2 tablespoons olive oil
- 1 medium onion (chopped)
- 2 jalapeños (chopped)
- 1 habanero pepper (chopped)
- 2 cloves garlic (chopped)
- 1 pound ground beef
- 3 tablespoons brown sugar
- 2 tablespoons Worcestershire sauce
- 2 tablespoons spicy brown mustard
- 1 tablespoon paprika
- 2 tablespoons cayenne powder
- Salt and pepper
- 1 cup tomato sauce (any brand)
- 3 tablespoons apple cider vinegar
- 2 tablespoons hot sauce
- ½ cup smoked Gouda (shredded)
- Toasted sourdough slices

Instructions:

1. Add the olive oil to a large skillet over medium heat. Then, sauté the onion and both types of peppers for 5-6 minutes until soft.
2. Next, stir in the garlic and cook for 1 minute. Once the garlic is fragrant, add the ground beef to the pan and cook for 7-8 minutes, continually stirring until the meat is cooked through.
3. Stir in the brown sugar, Worcestershire sauce, spicy mustard, paprika, cayenne pepper, salt and pepper, tomato sauce, apple cider vinegar, and hot sauce. Allow to simmer for 15-20 minutes to allow the flavors to fuse and the Sloppy Joe sauce to thicken.
4. Preheat the main oven to 350 degrees F.
5. Ladle the Sloppy Joe sauce over the slices of toasted sourdough bread. Scatter smoked Gouda on top. Transfer to a baking sheet and place in the preheated oven to bake for 5-6 minutes, until the cheeses start to melt and bubble. Remove from the oven, top with a little more hot sauce to taste and serve.

Chapter II - Appetizers, Dips and Sides

(13) Wasabi Crab Patties

Bring the heat to these wicked crab cakes with Japanese horseradish—wasabi!

Serving Size: 24

Preparation Time: 35 minutes

Total Times: 45 minutes

Ingredient List:

- 1 medium sweet red pepper (finely chopped)
- 1 celery rib (finely chopped)
- ⅓ cup plus ½ cup dry bread crumbs (divided)
- 3 green onions (finely chopped)
- 2 egg whites
- 3 tablespoons fat-free mayonnaise
- ¼ teaspoon prepared wasabi
- 1½ cups lump crabmeat (drained)
- Cooking spray

For the sauce

- 1 celery rib (finely chopped)
- ⅓ cup fat-free mayonnaise
- 1 green onion (finely chopped)
- 1 tablespoon sweet pickle relish
- ½ tsp prepared wasabi

Instructions:

1. Preheat the main oven to 425 degrees F.
2. In a large bowl, combine the red pepper, chopped celery, 1/3 cup breadcrumbs, green onions, egg whites, mayonnaise, and wasabi. Gently fold in the lump crab.
3. Place the remaining ½ cup of breadcrumbs in a small dish. Drop a heaped tablespoonful of the crab mixtures into the dish with the crumbs. Gently, coat and mold the mixture into ¾" thick patties. Place the patties on a rimless baking sheet lightly coated with cooking spray. Repeat the process until all the mixture has been used.
4. Spray the patties with cooking spray and bake in the preheated oven for 15-18 minutes. They are ready when they are golden brown. Make sure you turn them once or twice during the cooking process.
5. To make the sauce: Combine all the sauce ingredients in a small bowl. Stir thoroughly and serve with the crab patties.

(14) Cajun Wings

Enjoy a taste of the South with these Cajun seasoned hot wings. Serving with a creamy dip will help to take a little heat out of these spicy devils.

Serving Size: 6

Preparation Time: 20 minutes

Total Cooking Time: 1 hour 20 minutes

Ingredient List:

- 2½ pounds chicken wings
- 1 cup hot sauce
- 2 tablespoons chili paste
- ¼ cup salted butter (melted)
- 1 tablespoon Cajun seasoning
- 1 teaspoon vinegar
- ½ teaspoon sea salt

Instructions:

1. Place all of the chicken wings in a ziplock bag.
2. In a medium mixing bowl, combine the hot sauce, chili paste, butter, Cajun seasoning, vinegar, and sea salt. Hold back half of the mixture to use later. Pour the remaining marinade into the zipper bag. Seal the bag and gently massage to coat the chicken. Allow the bag to rest at room temperature for 45 minutes.
3. Preheat the main oven to 375 degrees F. Line a baking tin or pan with aluminum foil.
4. Take the wings out of the zipper bag, shake off, and discard any excess marinade. Lay the chicken wings on a foil-lined baking pan. Bake in the preheated oven for 30 minutes. Turn the wings over and bake for another 30 minutes. The wings are cooked when there is no visible pink meat and the juices run clear.
5. Remove the wings from the oven and transfer to the medium bowl containing the remaining marinade mixture. Toss in the marinade to coat.

(15) Hot 'n Spicy Crab Dip

A super tasty dip to serve with crisp crackers or raw vegetable sticks. Pairs perfectly with celery and cucumber. Simple to make and ideal for a large party or group.

Serving Size: 32

Preparation Time: 15 minutes

Total Cooking Time: 15 minutes

Ingredient List:

- ⅓ cup mayonnaise
- 2 tablespoons dried onion (minced)
- 2 tablespoons lemon juice
- 2 tablespoons white wine
- 1 tablespoon garlic (minced)
- ½ teaspoon cayenne pepper
- ½ teaspoon hot pepper sauce
- 16 ounces cream cheese (cubed)
- 1 pound imitation crab meat (chopped)

Instructions:

1. In a blender or food processor, combine all the ingredients apart from the crabmeat. Blitz until silky. Transfer the mixture to a large, microwave-safe bowl. Add the crabmeat and stir thoroughly.
2. Cover the bowl and microwave until the mixture lightly bubbles—this should take about 3 minutes.
3. Serve warm and enjoy!

(16) Spicy Welsh Rarebit

A variation of the hearty appetizer, direct from Wales, this one's for all the cheese lovers out there.

Serving Size: 2

Preparation Time: 10 minutes

Total Cooking Time: 25 minutes

Ingredient List:

- 2 large flat mushrooms
- 2 tablespoons olive oil
- 1 garlic clove (finely chopped)
- 1 small handful of fresh thyme
- 1 handful strong Cheddar cheese (grated)
- ½ red chili pepper
- 1 egg
- Salt and pepper
- 2 slices of thick crusty bread (toasted)
- Hot sauce

Ingredient List:

1. Preheat the main oven to 350 degrees F.
2. Lay the flat mushrooms on a baking sheet or tray and drizzle each mushroom with olive oil, garlic, and thyme. Bake for approximately 12-15 minutes, or until softened.
3. In the meantime, combine the grated cheese, chili pepper, egg, salt, and pepper. Stir well until totally mixed. Spoon the mixture evenly onto each individual mushroom and place under a hot grill along with 2 slices of thick, crusty bread. The

mushrooms are ready to serve when the cheese bubbles and starts to turn golden brown.
4. Serve the mixture on the toast with a generous dash of hot sauce.

(17) Curried Coconut Egg Drop Soup

A Chinese soup made with wispy eggs beaten into simmering chicken broth. A lighter option.

Serving Size: 1

Preparation Time: 10 minutes

Total Cooking Time: 20 minutes

Ingredient List:

- ½ cup chicken stock

- ½ cup coconut milk
- 1 green onion (finely chopped)
- 1 tablespoon fresh cilantro (chopped)
- ⅛ teaspoon curry powder
- ⅛ teaspoon chili powder
- ¼ teaspoon ground ginger
- 1 large egg (beaten)
- Black pepper

Instructions:

1. In a large saucepan, combine the chicken stock, coconut milk, onion, cilantro, curry powder, chili powder, and ground ginger. Stir and bring to a boil. Then, lower the heat and bring down to simmer.
2. Slowly and carefully drizzle the beaten egg into the soup in fine, ribbon-like strands. Using a fork, whisk well until the egg is thoroughly cooked; this should take no more than 3 minutes. Sprinkle with black pepper and serve.

(18) Spicy Bacon-Wrapped Shrimp

A delicious appetizer for any occasion.

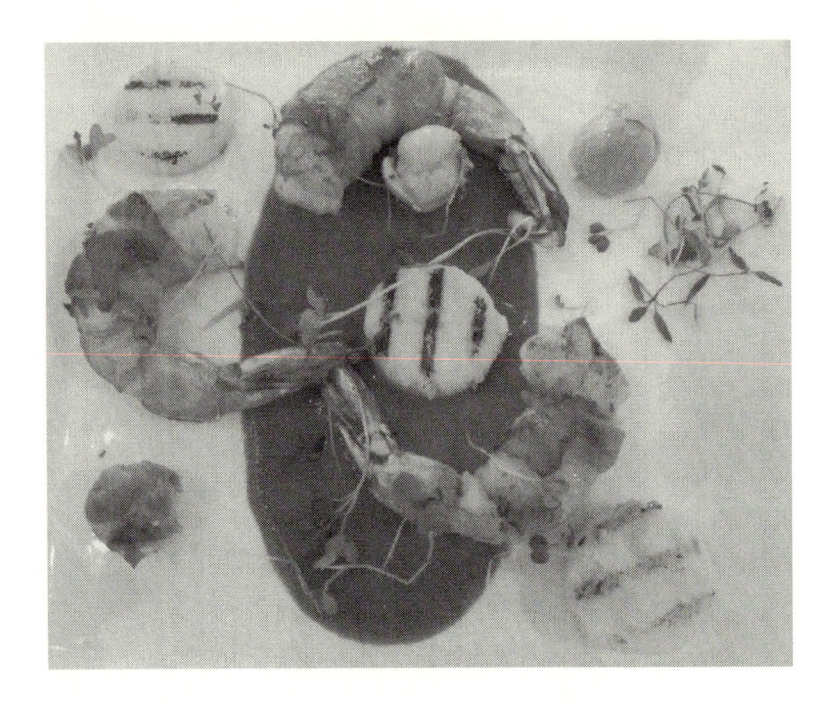

Serving Size: 6

Preparation Time: 15 minutes

Total Cooking Time: 1 hour 30 minutes

Ingredients

- ¼ cup sugar
- ¼ cup fresh lemon juice
- 2 tablespoons virgin olive oil
- 4 teaspoons paprika
- 1 teaspoon sea salt
- 1 teaspoon black pepper
- 1 teaspoon each of cayenne pepper, hot curry powder, ground cumin and ground cilantro
- 18 uncooked jumbo shrimps (peeled, deveined)
- 9 bacon strips (cut in half, lengthwise)

Instructions:

1. In a medium mixing bowl, combine the sugar, lemon juice, olive oil, and all the seasonings, herbs, and spices. Pour ¼ cup of the mixture into a re-sealable zipper bag and add the jumbo shrimp. Zip the bag closed and gently massage to coat all the shrimp. Place the bag in the refrigerator for 45-60 minutes. Cover the remaining marinade mixture and place in the refrigerator as well (you will be using it later for basting).
2. In a large frying pan or skillet, cook the bacon strips over medium heat. They should be cooked through, but not crispy. Take the bacon out of the pan and pat it with kitchen paper to remove any excess oil.
3. Remove the shrimp from the zipper bag and discard the marinade mixture. Wrap each individual shrimp with a piece of cooked bacon and place a cocktail stick through its center to secure.
4. Lightly moisten a paper towel with a little oil and coat the grill rack. Lay the shrimp parcels on the rack. Cover with aluminum foil and grill the shrimp on a medium heat, until they turn pink. This should take 7-10 minutes. Turn and baste a couple of times with the remaining marinade.

(19) Firecracker Chicken Meatballs

You may need to serve these meatballs with a cool dip or mayonnaise dressing. They are hot, hot, hot!

Serving Size: 20-24

Preparation Time: 15 minutes

Total Cooking Time: 2 hours 10 minutes

Ingredient List:

- 2 pounds ground chicken
- 1½ cups breadcrumbs
- 2 medium eggs
- ¼ cup white onion (finely chopped)
- 3 garlic cloves (minced)
- 1 tablespoon fresh parsley (chopped)
- Kosher salt and black pepper (to taste)
- ½ cup buffalo sauce (any brand)
- ½ cup brown sugar
- 2 tablespoons soy sauce
- Fresh parsley (chopped, for garnish)
- Red pepper flakes (for serving)

Instructions:

1. In a large bowl, mix the ground chicken with breadcrumbs, eggs, chopped onion, minced garlic, and one tablespoon of parsley. Stir well to fully combine and season with salt and black pepper to taste.
2. Using disposable gloves, mold the mixture into small evenly sized balls. The quantities should yield between 20 and 24 individual meatballs.
3. Line a baking tin or tray with aluminum foil, spray it with a little cooking spray, and arrange the meatballs on the tin so that they do not touch one another. Brown the meatballs on a high heat under the grill for 5-6 minutes each side. Flip them over during cooking to ensure that they are cooked all the way through.
4. Transfer to a slow cooker and add the store-bought buffalo sauce, brown sugar, and soy sauce.
5. Cook on a low setting for about 2 hours. When you are ready to serve, scatter the meatballs with fresh parsley and lots of red pepper flakes.

(20) Spiced Spinach and Onion Pakoras

Pakora is a common street food enjoyed throughout India. These fried snacks are delicious served with a fruit or onion chutney.

Serving Size: 16-20

Preparation Time: 10 minutes

Total Cooking Time: 30 minutes

Ingredient List:

- 2 cups chickpea flour
- 1 cup spinach leaves (chopped)
- 1 cup natural yogurt
- ½ cup cold water
- 1 tablespoon ground cilantro
- 1 tablespoon ground cumin
- 1 tablespoon dried fenugreek leaves (crushed)
- 1 large white onion (sliced thinly)
- Sea salt
- 2 cups vegetable oil

Instructions:

1. In a large mixing bowl, combine the chickpea flour, spinach leaves, yogurt, water, cilantro, cumin, fenugreek, and sliced onions. Season well with salt and stir well until totally mixed.
2. Using a heavy large pot, heat the vegetable oil to around 350 degrees F.
3. Taking care not to splash, spoon the batter into the hot oil and deep fry. Work in batches, until each pakora rises to the surface. They are cooked when they are golden brown in color. This should take 4-5 minutes.
4. Remove from the oil and drain on a baking rack lined with paper towels. Sprinkle each pakora with a little sea salt and enjoy!

(21) Honey Ginger Shrimp

Sweet honey fuses with spicy ginger to give these shrimps the kick they deserve! Enjoy straight from the pan.

Serving Size: 4

Preparation Time: 10 minutes

Total Cooking Time: 20 minutes

Ingredient List:

- 2 tablespoons olive oil
- 1 tablespoon red pepper flakes
- ¼ yellow onion (chopped)
- 1 teaspoon garlic (chopped)
- 1 teaspoon ground ginger
- 1 teaspoon honey
- 1 pound medium shrimp (peeled, deveined)
- Salt and black pepper

Instructions:

1. In a large frying pan or skillet on medium-high, heat the olive oil. Add the red pepper flakes, onions, garlic, ginger, and finally the honey. Stir well to combine. Next, add the shrimp and fry for 4-5 minutes. Continue stirring until the shrimp have turned a pink color and are opaque.
2. Serve hot, seasoned with salt and black pepper, and enjoy immediately.

(22) Prawn Puri

Impress your friends with this spicy prawn puri, then follow it with a hot, home cooked spicy curry. Serve with a green salad and have plenty of chilled water on hand for thirsty diners.

Serving Size: 4

Preparation Time: 10 minutes

Total Cooking Time: 35 minutes

Ingredient List:

- 3 tablespoons ghee
- 28 ounces small fresh peeled prawns
- 2 medium onions (finely chopped)
- 2 tomatoes (finely chopped)
- 3 green chilies (finely chopped)
- 1 tablespoon garam masala
- 1 teaspoon ground cumin
- Salt
- Juice of 2 limes
- 1 small bunch coriander (finely chopped)
- 4 readymade frozen puri bread (thawed, warmed)

Instructions:

1. In a large, heavy-bottomed frying pan or wok, heat 1 tablespoon of ghee. When the ghee is very hot, add the peeled prawns; cook until they are browned on the outside but only two-thirds cooked on the inside. Remove the partially cooked prawns from the pan and set aside.
2. Add the remaining 2 tablespoonss of ghee to the pan along with the chopped onions. Toss and fry, making sure to constantly stir. The onions are cooked when they become translucent; this should take 4-5 minutes.
3. Next, add the chopped tomatoes. Then add the green chilies, garam masala, cumin, and a little salt. Stir well.
4. Add the cooked prawns and make sure that the liquid covers them fully. If it doesn't, add a little more water.
5. Finally, add the lime juice and scatter with coriander. Spoon on top of warmed puri bread.

(23) Horseradish Cream Cheese with Fruit Dip

A zesty dip that is simple to make and great coupled with warm bread or crackers.

Serving Size: 10

Preparation Time: 10 minutes

Total Cooking Time: 10 minutes

Ingredient List:

- 8 ounces fat- free cream cheese
- ⅓ cup apple jelly (warmed)
- 1 tablespoon prepared horseradish
- 1½ teaspoon ground mustard
- ⅓ cup apricot fruit spread

Instructions:

1. Place the cream cheese on a serving platter.
2. In a microwave-safe bowl, warm the apple jelly. Add the horseradish and ground mustard and stir until well combined. Finally, add the apricot spread and stir again.
3. Spoon the dip over the cream cheese and serve.

(24) Mexican Chili Grilled Corn

Serving grilled corn is a great way to get a barbecue off to a good start. Not too heavy and not too filling—a great appetite teaser.

Serving Size: 4

Preparation Time: 5 minutes

Total Cooking Time: 25 minutes

Ingredient List:

- 4 ears corn
- ½ cup full-fat mayonnaise
- 1½ cups sour cream
- ¼ cup fresh cilantro leaves (chopped)
- 1 cup fresh Parmesan (grated)
- Juice of 1 lime
- Red chili powder

Instructions:

1. First, prepare the corn by removing the husks. However, you should leave the cores attached as it makes handling easier.
2. Using a cast iron skillet, grill the corn on a high heat until it is a little charred. Turn the corn over so that it is cooked evenly.
3. In a bowl, combine the mayonnaise, sour cream, and chopped cilantro. Mix well.
4. While the corn is warm, dredge it in the mayo mixture. Squeeze a little lime juice over each corn ear and scatter with Parmesan. Season well with red chili powder and serve!

(25) Horseradish Deviled Eggs

Colorful, flavorful, and packed full of hot seasonings. A tasty appetizer or a light snack.

Serving Size: 6

Preparation Time: 15 minutes

Total Cooking Time: 15 minutes

Ingredients

- 6 large eggs, hard-boiled
- ¼ cup mayonnaise
- 2 tablespoons prepared horseradish
- ½ teaspoon dill weed
- ¼ teaspoon ground mustard
- ⅛ teaspoon salt
- ¼ teaspoon black pepper
- ¼ teaspoon paprika

Instructions:

1. Cut each egg in half lengthwise. Then take out the yolks and place them in a medium sized bowl. Keep the egg white halves intact—you are going to fill them later—and set to one side.
2. Using a fork, mash the 6 yolks. Add the mayonnaise, horseradish, dill weed, ground mustard, salt, and black pepper. Stir well to combine.
3. Evenly spoon the mixture into each egg white's cavity. Sprinkle each filled egg with a little paprika and chill in the refrigerator prior to serving.

(26) Jalapeño Poppers

This recipe will yield about 32 crispy little poppers that melt in the mouth. But beware, your guests will feel the burn!

Serving Size: 32

Preparation Time: 45 minutes

Total Cooking Time: 1 hour

Ingredient List:

- 12 ounces full-fat cream cheese (softened)
- 8 ounces Cheddar cheese (shredded)
- 2 tablespoons bacon bits
- 16 jalapeños (seeded, halved)
- 1 cup whole milk
- 1 cup all-purpose flour
- 1 cup panko breadcrumbs
- 2 quarts oil

Instructions:

1. In a medium bowl, combine the cream cheese, grated Cheddar, and bacon bits. Spoon the mixture into the jalapeño pepper halves.
2. Place the milk and flour into two separate bowls. Dip each jalapeño first into the bowl containing the milk, then in the flour. Each jalapeño needs to be evenly and well coated with both ingredients. Set the jalapeños aside to dry for 8-10 minutes.
3. When dry, once again dip the jalapeños into the milk, and then roll each carefully in breadcrumbs. Again, allow to dry. Each of the jalapeños should be evenly coated.
4. Using a frying pan or skillet, heat the 2 quarts of oil and fry the jalapeños for 3-4 minutes each, until they are golden brown all over. Remove the jalapeños from the oil and pat dry with kitchen paper towel.
5. Serve hot with salsa.

(27) Hot Artichoke and Spinach Dip

Artichokes have a superb yet mild flavor. Combined with Italian cheeses, this makes an ideal appetizer to serve to guests on toasted bread.

Serving Size: 12

Preparation Time: 15 minutes

Total Cooking Time: 40 minutes

Ingredient List:

- 8 ounces cream cheese (softened)
- ¼ cup mayonnaise
- ¼ cup Parmesan cheese (grated)
- ¼ cup Romano cheese (grated)
- ½ teaspoon dried basil
- ¼ teaspoon garlic salt
- ½ cup frozen spinach (thawed, drained, chopped)
- 1 tablespoon prepared horseradish
- Salt and black pepper
- 14 ounces canned artichoke hearts (drained, chopped)
- ¼ cup mozzarella cheese (shredded)

Instructions:

1. Preheat the main oven to 350 degrees F. Lightly grease a medium sized baking tin or dish.
2. In a mixing bowl, combine the cream cheese, mayonnaise, Parmesan and Romano cheeses, basil, garlic salt, horseradish, and black pepper. Mix thoroughly before stirring in the drained artichoke hearts and chopped spinach.
3. Transfer the mixture to the greased baking tin. Scatter mozzarella cheese on top and bake in the preheated oven for 25-30 minutes. The dish is ready when the cheese bubbles and becomes a light golden brown.

Chapter III – Dessert

(28) Cranberry-Jalapeño Granita

Complex flavors define this sweet and spicy dessert, complimented with fresh lime and mint. It's a perfect palate cleanser and an after dinner favorite.

Serving Size: 4

Preparation Time: 10 minutes

Total Cooking Time: 4 hours 10 minutes

Ingredient List:

- 2 cups low-calorie cranberry juice cocktail
- ⅓ cup sugar
- 4 mint sprigs
- 1 jalapeño chili (sliced)
- 2 tablespoons fresh lime juice

Instructions:

1. Combine the cranberry juice, sugar, mint, and chili in a medium saucepan and bring to a boil. Cover the pan, remove from the heat, and allow to rest for 15 minutes.
2. Strain the cranberry mixture through a sieve into a baking dish (11x7"), discarding the solids. Allow the mixture to cool to around room temperature. Add the lime juice. Stir to fully combine.
3. Cover the baking dish and transfer to the freezer for 3 hours, or until completely frozen solid. Stir the mixture every 45 minutes.
4. When frozen, remove from the fridge and scuff up the entire granita using a fork.

(29) Wasabi Pea Chocolate Bark

These chocolate nibbles combine the sultry richness of dark chocolate with the fiery heat of Japanese wasabi.

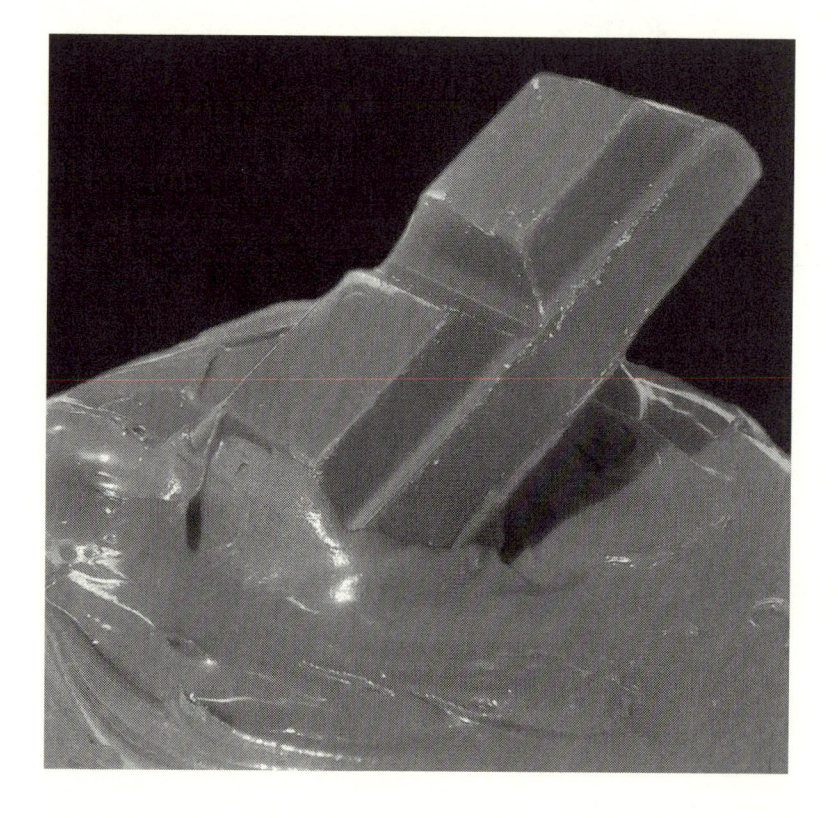

Serving Size: 4

Preparation Time: 8 minutes

Total Cooking Time: 30 minutes

Hot & Spicy Cookbook - 88

Ingredient List:

- 3 ½ ounces dark chocolate
- ½ cup wasabi peas and Asian rice cracker mix
- Pinch of sea salt

Instructions:

1. Using a heat proof bowl, melt the dark chocolate in the microwave for 35-45 second intervals. Stir in between heating until the chocolate has totally melted.
2. Line a rimless baking tray or sheet with greaseproof paper. Spread the melted chocolate on the sheet in a single layer.
3. In a resealable ziplock bag, combine 2 tablespoonss of wasabi mix and a couple of rice crackers. Lightly crush them using a mallet. Scatter the remaining wasabi and rice cracker mix on top of the chocolate layer. Next, sprinkle with the crushed mixture from the zipper bag and a little sea salt.
4. Cool the wasabi bark in the refrigerator. Break into irregular pieces and enjoy!

(30) Apple Dutch Baby with Green Chilis

Another name for a Dutch baby is German pancake, which is a little bit like a crepe. This recipe combines sharp apples with spicy chilis.

Serving Size: 4-8

Preparation Time: 5 minutes

Total Cooking Time: 20 minutes

Ingredient List:

- 4 tablespoons unsalted butter
- 2 firm cooking apples (peeled, cored, thinly sliced)
- ¼ cup granulated sugar
- ¼ teaspoon ground cinnamon
- ½ teaspoon salt
- 4 large eggs
- 1 cup milk
- 1 cup all-purpose flour
- ½ teaspoon vanilla extract
- 1 jalapeño chili (stemmed, seeded, diced)
- 1 tablespoon powdered sugar

Instructions:

1. Preheat the oven to 425 degrees F.
2. On a low heat in an ovenproof cast iron skillet, melt the unsalted butter. Add the apples, sugar, cinnamon, and salt to the pan and cook for 8-10 minutes until softened. Stir only occasionally.
3. In the meantime, combine the eggs, milk, all-purpose flour, and vanilla extract in a blender and blitz until a smooth batter is formed.
4. Once the apples are softened, scatter them with diced jalapeño chilis and pour the mixture over the batter.
5. Bake the skillet, with no lid, in the preheated oven until puffy and until a knife inserted in the center of the pancake comes out clean. This should take about 15 minutes.
6. Sprinkle with sugar and enjoy.

(31) Tequila Grilled Watermelon

The ultimate summer dessert. Refreshing watermelon spiked with tequila and laced with hot chili!

Serving Size: 4

Preparation Time: 3 minutes

Total Cooking Time: 10 minutes

Ingredient List:

- 2 shots good quality tequila
- 1 tablespoon sea salt
- 1 lemon (zest and juice)
- 3 teaspoons ancho chili powder
- 8 ounces crème fraiche
- Zest of 1 fresh lime
- ⅓ cup fresh cilantro (roughly chopped)
- 4 square chunks fresh watermelon

Instructions:

1. Combine the tequila, sea salt, lemon zest and juice, and chili powder in a bowl. Set aside for a moment.
2. Combine the crème fraiche, lime zest, and cilantro in a separate bowl and stir. Set aside.
3. Dunk each square of watermelon in the tequila mixture before placing on the grill. Grill on one side only until the melon is scored.
4. Serve the melon with a generous dollop of the lime/cilantro crème fraiche.

(32) Black Pepper Ice-Cream

If you like your ice cream hot, you will love this recipe!

Serving Size: 6-8

Preparation Time: 50 minutes

Total Cooking Time: 2 hours 50 minutes

Ingredient List:

- 1½ cups milk
- 1½ cups heavy cream
- 1 tablespoon black peppercorns (whole)
- 2 teaspoons black pepper (ground)
- 4 black cardamom pods
- 3 green cardamom pods (crushed)
- 6 eggs yolks
- ⅔ cup sugar
- Cracked pepper

Instructions:

1. In a medium-size saucepan over low heat, warm the milk, cream, seasoning, and spices for 35 minutes.
2. In a medium sized bowl whisk the 6 egg yolks into the sugar until totally combined. Temper the egg yolks, taking care not to scramble them, into the milk and cream. Cook until the mixture is thick enough to coat the back of a tablespoon.
3. Take the pan off the heat and allow to cool.
4. Transfer to an ice cream maker and freeze according to the individual manufacturer's instructions.
5. Serve, sprinkled with a little cracked pepper.

(33) Strawberry and Jalapeño Gin Popsicles

Dessert on a stick. An after-dinner tipple, definitely for adult guests only!

Serving Size: 8-10

Preparation Time: 10 minutes

Total Cooking Time: 8 hours 10 minutes

Ingredient List:

- 1 pound fresh strawberries (chopped)
- 1 jalapeño (finely chopped)
- 3-5 tablespoons white sugar
- 1½ cup fresh lime juice
- ¾ cup good quality gin

Instructions:

1. In a flat-bottomed, shallow dish or bowl, mash the strawberries and diced jalapeño. Transfer the mixture to a small saucepan over medium heat, stir, and bring to a boil. Stir continuously and allow to remain boiling for 2 ½ minutes.
2. Remove the pan from the heat and cool. Once completely cooled, add the lime juice and gin and stir.
3. Pour the mixture into individual popsicle molds. Cover with aluminum foil and pop a stick in the center of each mold.
4. Freeze overnight.

(34) Cardamom and Vanilla Ice Cream

It is not unusual to use Cardamom in ice cream in the Middle East and India.

Serving Size: 6

Preparation Time: 40 minutes

Total Cooking Time: 4 hours 40 minutes

Ingredient List:

- 2 cups milk
- 1 vanilla bean (split lengthwise)
- 8 whole green cardamom pods (lightly crushed)
- ¾ cup sugar
- 4 egg yolks
- ¾ cup whipping cream
- ⅛ teaspoon ground cardamom

Instructions:

1. Add the milk, vanilla bean, and cardamom pods to a large pan and slowly bring to the boil. Once boiling, remove from the heat, cover the pan with a lid and allow the mixture to infuse for 25 minutes. Remove the vanilla bean and scrape the seeds in to the mixture. Discard the cardamom pods.
2. In a medium bowl, beat the egg yolks and sugar together until you achieve a thick consistency. Slowly reheat the milk mixture and beat a small amount of it into the yolks. Then, pour the egg mixture into the milk and return it back to the saucepan on low heat.
3. Stir continuously until the custard is thick enough to coat the back of a tablespoon. This should take 5-7 minutes. Keep the heat low. Do not allow the mixture to scramble.
4. Remove the saucepan from the heat and stir until nearly cool.

5. In a small bowl, whisk the whipping cream and gradually fold it into the custard. Stir in the ground cardamom.
6. Transfer the custard to an ice cream maker. Freeze according to the individual manufacturer's instructions.

(35) Spicy Peanut Popcorn

Game on! Hot and spicy caramel corn that adults will love to nibble. Delicious before and after a meal or as a light snack in between.

Serving Size: 12

Preparation Time: 30 minutes

Total Cooking Time: 1 hour 30 minutes

Ingredient List:

For the spicy peanuts

- 2 ½ cups roasted, unsalted peanuts
- ¼ cup light corn syrup
- 2 tablespoons brown sugar
- 1 ½ teaspoon kosher salt
- 1 teaspoon chili powder
- ½ teaspoon cayenne pepper

For the caramel corn

- 10 cups freshly popped popcorn (no added sugar/salt/fat)
- 1 stick unsalted butter
- 1 cup packed dark brown sugar
- ½ cup light corn syrup
- ½ teaspoon coarse kosher salt
- ¼ teaspoon baking soda
- ½ teaspoon pure vanilla extract

Instructions:

1. Preheat the main oven to 350 degrees F. Line a rimless baking tray or sheet with greaseproof paper.
2. In a large bowl, combine the peanuts, corn syrup, brown sugar, kosher salt, chili powder, and cayenne pepper. Toss the bowl until the peanuts are all coated. Transfer the peanuts to the baking tray. Bake for about 15 minutes, occasionally stirring. The peanuts around the outside edges of the pan should begin to darken.
3. Allow the peanuts to cool. They should now have a brittle-like appearance. Break this brittle into bite sized chunks. Set to one side.
4. To make the caramel corn: Preheat the main oven to 200 degrees F. Line a rimless baking tray or sheet with greaseproof paper.
5. Take a medium saucepan and combine the brown sugar, corn syrup, and kosher salt. Bring the pan to a boil over medium heat. Using a candy thermometer, to monitor the temperature, stir until the mixture reaches 238 degrees F. Once this heat is reached, remove the pan from the heat and add the baking soda and vanilla extract. Stir to combine.

6. In a large mixing bowl, combine the popcorn and the peanut brittle chunks set aside a little earlier.
7. Carefully pour the hot caramel over the popcorn and peanuts. Toss well until evenly coated. Transfer the popcorn mixture to the baking tray and bake for 20 minutes. Stir and continue to bake for a further 20 minutes.
8. If you store the corn in an airtight container with a lid, it will keep fresh for up to 3 weeks.

(36) Chocolate Chili Pots

Inspired by the flavors of Mexico, chocolate and chili combine to deliver a decadent dessert in a pot.

Serving Size: 6

Preparation Time: 10 minutes

Total Cooking Time: 5 hours 10 minutes

Ingredient List:

- 1 ancho chili
- 1¼ cups pouring cream
- 8 ounces dark chocolate (roughly chopped)
- 3 egg yolks (lightly beaten)
- 2 tablespoons white sugar
- 1 ounce unsalted butter (softened)
- 1 teaspoon dried chili flakes

Instructions:

1. In a small saucepan over the medium heat, combine the ancho chili and pouring cream. Bring to a boil. Remove the pan from the heat and discard the ancho chili.
2. Add the dark chocolate, continuously stirring until the chocolate is silky smooth. Set to one side to cool. When cool, whisk in the beaten egg yolks, white sugar, and unsalted butter. Stir well until combined.
3. Transfer the chocolate mixture to 6 individual ramekins. Place the ramekins in the refrigerator and chill for at least 1 hour. Scatter the top of each dessert with chili flakes and chill for an additional 3-4 hours until set.

(37) Fire Roasted Pears

Hot sauce pairs perfectly with lots of different fruits!

Serving Size: 4

Preparation Time: 5 minutes

Total Cooking Time: 30 minutes

Ingredient List:

- 4 large ripe pears
- ⅓ cup chopped walnuts
- 3 tablespoons brown sugar
- 3 tablespoons butter (softened)
- ¾ teaspoon hot sauce
- ¼ teaspoon ground cinnamon
- Drops of hot sauce

Instructions:

1. Preheat the grill to medium heat.
2. Slice the top off each pear (1" below the stem) and set aside for later. Core the pears using a spoon. You will be filling the cavity later.
3. In a small bowl, combine the chopped walnuts, brown sugar, butter, hot sauce, and ground cinnamon. Add one further drop of hot sauce to each pear cavity. Spoon the walnut mixture equally into the cavities of the 4 pears. Replace the top on each of the pears.
4. Transfer the filled pears to a lightly greased 9" square of heavy aluminum foil. Place the foil on the grill and roast the pears until tender. This should take 20-25 minutes depending on the size and ripeness of the fruit.

(38) Chocolate Dipped Coconut Curry Macaroons

These sweet and spicy macaroon morsels will have everyone coming back for more.

Serving Size: 20

Preparation Time: 15 minutes

Total Cooking Time: 1 hour 35 minutes

Ingredient List:

- Macaroons
- 2 cups sweetened coconut flakes
- 1 large egg white
- 2 teaspoons Madras curry powder
- ¼ teaspoon turmeric
- ¼ teaspoon salt
- ¾ cup sweetened condensed milk
- Chocolate ganache
- 6 ounces semisweet chocolate chips
- ½ cup plus 2 tablespoons heavy cream
- Pinch of fine salt

Instructions:

Preheat the main over to 350 degrees F.

1. In a medium bowl, beat the egg white to form stiff peaks. Sift in the Madras curry powder, turmeric, and salt. Gently fold until combined.
2. Gently fold the coconut flakes into the egg white mixture. Mix thoroughly and pour in the condensed milk. Stir well.
3. Using an ice cream scoop or similar size utensil, spoon the mixture onto a cookie sheet lined with greaseproof paper.
4. Bake in the preheated oven until golden. This should take 15-20 minutes.
5. Remove from oven and allow to cool on a wire rack.
6. For the ganache: Pour the chocolate chips into a small dish.
7. Warm the heavy cream in a small saucepan over medium heat. Remove the cream from the heat just before it reaches boiling and pour it over the chocolate chips. Sprinkle with fine salt and allow to stand for 5 minutes. Stir well until the ganache is silky.

8. Gently pick up each macaroon with a fork and dip it in the ganache. Transfer each chocolate dipped macaroon to greaseproof paper. Repeat until all of the macaroons have been chocolate coated.
9. Transfer the macaroons to the refrigerator to set for approximately 30-40 minutes.
10. Allow to come to room temperature before serving.

(39) Dark Chocolate Jalapeño Bread Pudding

Add a little spice to a warm bread pudding for a satisfying dessert.

Serving Size: 4

Preparation Time: 10 minutes

Total Cooking Time: 1 hour 10 minutes

Ingredient List:

- Butter (for greasing)
- 3 tablespoons unsalted butter
- 2½ cups whole milk
- ¼ cup granulated sugar
- 1½ cups semi-sweet chocolate chips (divided)
- 14 jalapeño rolls (any brand)
- ¾ cup dried cherries
- ½ cup walnuts (chopped)
- 2 large eggs
- 1 teaspoon vanilla extract
- 1 teaspoon ancho chile powder
- ⅛ teaspoon sea salt

Instructions:

1. Preheat the main oven to 350 degrees F. Lightly grease a baking dish (2 quart) with butter.

2. In a medium saucepan over medium heat, melt the unsalted butter. Stir in the milk and sugar. Bring to a gentle simmer, stirring continuously until the granules of sugar are completely dissolved.

3. Remove the saucepan from the heat and add just 1 cup of the semi-sweet chocolate chips. Allow the pan to rest for 5-7 minutes, before whisking until the chocolate is silky. While you are waiting for the chocolate to melt, add the rolls to the baking dish. Sprinkle the cherries on top of the rolls along with the walnuts and the remaining chips.

4. Next, whisk in the eggs, vanilla, ancho powder, and salt to the milk-chocolate mixture. When both mixtures are totally combined, pour them into the baking dish and allow the ingredients to rest for a few minutes to allow the milk to soak into the rolls.

5. Bake in the preheated oven for 40-45 minutes. Test that it is ready by inserting a knife into the very middle of the cake. If the knife doesn't come out clean pop back into the oven for a few more minutes. The center should be slightly moist but not wet.

6. Serve warm and enjoy.

(40) Chocolate Dipped Strawberries

These delightful strawberry treats are great to serve at a dinner party. Plus, they make a great alternative to after dinner mints.

Serving Size: 2-4

Preparation Time: 10 minutes

Total Cooking Time: 50 minutes

Ingredient List:

- 6 ounces bittersweet chocolate (chopped)
- 3 tablespoons heavy cream
- 1 tablespoon butter
- ⅛ teaspoon ancho powder
- 10 large strawberries (with stems)

Instructions:

1. Add the chocolate, heavy cream, and butter to a medium sized, heat resistant mixing bowl. Place the bowl over a small pan of boiling water. The base of the bowl must be larger than the pan, as you do not want the hot water to come into contact with the bottom of the bowl. Stir well until all of the chopped chocolate is totally melted and smooth. Add the ancho powder and combine fully.
2. Take each strawberry by its stem and carefully dip it into the melted chocolate. Hold it over the pan to ensure that any excess is not lost.
3. Transfer each dipped strawberry onto greaseproof paper and allow to cool. Once cool, place in the refrigerator until the chocolate sets, about 25 minutes.

About the Author

Nancy Silverman is an accomplished chef from Essex, Vermont. Armed with her degree in Nutrition and Food Sciences from the University of Vermont, Nancy has excelled at creating e-books that contain healthy and delicious meals that anyone can make and everyone can enjoy. She improved her cooking skills at the New England Culinary Institute in Montpelier Vermont and she has been working at perfecting her culinary style since graduation. She claims that her life's work is always a work in progress and she only hopes to be an inspiration to aspiring chefs everywhere.

Her greatest joy is cooking in her modern kitchen with her family and creating inspiring and delicious meals. She often says that she has perfected her signature dishes based on her family's critique of each and every one.

Nancy has her own catering company and has also been fortunate enough to be head chef at some of Vermont's most exclusive restaurants. When a friend suggested she share some of her outstanding signature dishes, she decided to add cookbook author to her repertoire of personal achievements. Being a technological savvy woman, she felt the e-book realm would be a better fit and soon she had her first cookbook available online. As of today, Nancy has sold over 1,000 e-books and has shared her culinary experiences and brilliant recipes with people from all over the world! She plans on expanding into self-help books and dietary cookbooks, so stayed tuned!

Author's Afterthoughts

Thank you for making the decision to invest in one of my cookbooks! I cherish all my readers and hope you find joy in preparing these meals as I have.

There are so many books available and I am truly grateful that you decided to buy this one and follow it from beginning to end.

I love hearing from my readers on what they thought of this book and any value they received from reading it. As a personal favor, I would appreciate any feedback you can give in the form of a review on Amazon and please be honest! This kind of support will help others make an informed choice on and will help me tremendously in producing the best quality books possible.

My most heartfelt thanks,

Nancy Silverman

If you're interested in more of my books, be sure to follow my author page on Amazon (can be found on the link Bellow) or scan the QR-Code.

https://www.amazon.com/author/nancy-silverman

Made in the USA
Columbia, SC
16 December 2024